The Story of
NOAH and

By REV. JUDE WINKLER, OFM Conv.

Imprimi Potest: Daniel Pietrzak, OFM Conv., Minister Provincial of St. Anthony of Padua Province (USA)
Nihil Obstat: James T. O'Connor, S.T.D., Censor Librorum
Imprimatur: Patrick J. Sheridan, Vicar General, Archdiocese of New York

The Nihil Obstat and Imprimatur are official declarations that a book or pamphlet is free of doctrinal or moral error. No implication is contained therein that those who have granted the Nihil Obstat and Imprimatur agree with the contents, opinions or statements expressed.

King David's court

DAVID was the greatest king that the people of Israel ever had. He was a great hero who defeated all of their enemies. He was a great friend to all, even the poor and the weak.

David was also a good friend of God. He tried to do what God wanted. When he made a mistake and turned away from God, he would always turn back to Him and ask His forgiveness.

He built a great palace in Jerusalem. He invited people from all over the world to come there so that he could show them all that God had done for Israel and for himself. Thus, they would know that the God of Israel, Yahweh, was the most powerful God.

David loved to hear about all the great things that God had done for the people of Israel throughout the ages. He would ask his storytellers to speak to him about Yahweh and how He loved His people. He especially wanted to hear of how Yahweh had mercy on His people when they sinned.

One day David's storytellers decided to tell him about the early days of the world. This was a story about God's goodness, our sinfulness, and God's love, which conquers even our sins.

The creation of man and woman

D AVID'S storytellers began to tell him of how God created the world. They spoke of God taking dust of the earth and forming it into the shape of a man. God then breathed into that man and gave him life.

God knew that this man should not be alone. He made this first man, Adam, fall into a deep sleep. He then took one of his ribs and out of it he formed woman. Adam gave this woman the name Eve.

God loved and cared for Adam and Eve. He placed them in the Garden of Eden and let them eat of the fruit of any of the trees in the garden except the tree of the knowledge of good and evil.

The devil came along and tempted Adam and Eve and convinced them to disobey the command that God had given them. Adam and Eve ate from the tree of the knowledge of good and evil. Then they realized that they had sinned, and they were afraid of God and hid themselves.

God spoke to them and told them that they had done wrong. He punished them for their sin and sent them out of the garden. Even then, though, He loved them, and He Himself made them some clothes to protect them from the cold.

Sin grows: the first murder

ADAM and Eve had two sons: Cain and Abel. Cain was a farmer and Abel was a shepherd. One day, both Cain and Abel decided to make a sacrifice to God. God accepted Abel's sacrifice, but he did not accept Cain's sacrifice. Cain was very jealous of Abel and angry at him.

God spoke to Cain and asked him why he was so angry. He warned Cain that he had to be careful for his anger could easily become a grave sin. But Cain did not want to listen to the Lord.

Cain invited Abel to go out to the field. When they arrived there and when he was sure that no one was looking, Cain killed his brother.

God later asked Cain where Abel was. Cain answered, "I do not know. Am I my brother's keeper?" God punished Cain for this terrible sin by sending him away to wander over the face of the earth. Even then, God still loved Cain, for He gave him a mark that would protect him from anyone who would want to harm him.

The sins of men and women continued to grow worse and worse. What began with Adam and Eve continued to grow like a terrible disease that covered the whole earth and everyone on it.

God decides to punish the earth

FINALLY, the world had become too evil for God to bear. He really loved the man and woman whom He had created and their children and their grandchildren, but He could no longer put up with their sins. The people He had created had become selfish and turned their backs on Him.

God decided that the only way for Him to do away with all of this sin was to destroy the world and to start over again. He would flood the entire world and kill all men and women, all animals of the fields and of the woods, all birds of the air— everything that He had created.

Yet God decided that He would not kill every single man and woman upon the earth. There was one family whom He decided that He would save: the family of Noah.

Noah was a good and upright man. He and his wife had three sons who were married, and Noah's family followed in the ways of the Lord.

God would save them from the terrible flood that He was about to bring upon the earth. Then, after the flood, they would become a new beginning for the human family, a beginning in goodness and love and not in sin.

God speaks to Noah

AND so God spoke to Noah one day. He told Noah all His plans, that He was going to put an end to life upon the earth because of all the sins that men and women had committed.

God told Noah that He did not want to harm him or his family. He told him that they had found favor in His sight and because of that He was going to save them from the flood that He was about to bring upon the earth.

God ordered Noah to build a large boat, which He called an ark. From the measurement that is given, it seems as if the ark looked like a large shoe box. Noah was very pleased that God had had mercy upon him. He listened carefully to all the instructions that God gave him on how he was to build the ark.

The ark was to be made out of gopherwood, and its entire inside and outside was to be covered with a type of tar. The tar would keep the water from coming into the ark through the cracks in the wood. It was to be three hundred cubits long, fifty cubits wide and thirty cubits high. That is about 450 feet long, 75 feet wide, and 45 feet high. It was to have three different layers and an entrance in its side.

Building the ark

NOAH immediately called together his sons, and they began to work on the ark. They worked all day long, for God had told them to work quickly for He was about to flood the earth.

As they worked on the boat, Noah's neighbors must have been surprised by what he was doing. They were so selfish and filled with sin that they would not listen to his warnings of what God was about to do. Instead, they probably made fun of Noah and his sons.

Noah's family continued with all their preparations for the great flood. While Noah and his sons built the ark, Noah's wife and his sons' wives gathered food, for they would be in the boat for a long time.

Whenever the work got heavy and they became tired, Noah would remind them of two things. One would frighten them: he would tell them to hurry, for the flood was coming soon. The other thing that Noah would say filled them with hope: he reminded them of the promise that God had made to them. God had told them that He would protect them throughout the flood and then after the flood He would make a Covenant (a promise of His special love) with them.

The final preparations

WHEN Noah and his sons had finished all their work on the ark, they realized that it was time to get aboard. Before they could do this, though, they had to go out and gather all kinds of animals from all over the world.

God had ordered them to bring these animals into the boat for He did not want to destroy all of the different kinds of animals in the flood. He was very happy with the animals that He had created, and He wanted them to survive the flood so that they might bring joy to Noah's family and to all of his descendants.

Noah and his family gathered males and females of each of the land animals and of the birds: any animal that might have died in the flood. When they had finished gathering all those animals, they brought them into the boat two by two.

Finally, all the animals were on the boat. Noah and his family then went into the boat themselves, just as God had commanded.

Noah was six hundred years old when he built the ark and brought his family aboard (for in those days men and women would live very long lives).

The rains begin

THE minute that Noah and his sons closed the entrance to the ark and sealed it with tar, it began to rain.

At first everyone thought that this was just a bad storm. It rained and it rained, day and night. It almost seemed as if the floodgates of heaven had been opened. And yet the people continued to sin and to do what was wrong in God's sight.

Meanwhile, Noah and his family knew what was happening. They thanked God for sparing them from the flood that was beginning, and they asked Him in His mercy to protect them.

After a few days, the flooding began. The first place to be flooded was the lowlands that would get flooded every rainy season. The people now knew that things were not normal, but they did not yet know how bad they would become.

The people on the land took their families and their belongings and moved to where there was higher ground. They felt confident that they were safe there, and as soon as they arrived they began to sin once again. They never thought of calling upon God for mercy because they did not want anything to do with God.

The flood covers all the land

AND yet it continued to rain. Some of the high places that had never before been covered in a flood were now deep under water. The people who were left began to climb the high hills, but soon they, too, were covered.

After a few more days, only the highest mountaintops were not covered, but it did not stop raining. The waters came pouring down until every piece of dry land was covered by the flood. As the flood rose, the people and the animals had no place to go, and they all drowned.

Even then it did not stop raining. In all, it rained for forty days and forty nights. The waters continued to rise until even the tops of the highest mountains were under more than twenty feet of water. The earth had never before seen a flood like this one.

Finally, after forty days and forty nights, it stopped raining. All the creatures that lived upon the face of the earth or in the skies had died except for Noah, his family, and the animals that they had brought aboard the ark.

Noah and his family continued to pray to God that He would save them from the terrible flood that He had brought upon the earth.

The flood dries up

EVEN when the rains finally stopped, the water did not go down immediately. The flood remained at its high point for one hundred and fifty days, about five months. Noah and his family and the animals had now been on the ark for over six months.

Then God decided that it was time to end His punishment of the earth. He had a great wind sweep over the face of the waters so that they could begin to dry up. At first Noah could not notice any change, but slowly he noticed that something was happening.

One day when quite a bit of the flood had dried up, the ark came to rest on a high mountain, one of the mountains of Ararat. Noah could still not see dry land, though, so he and his family remained in the ark. After a few more months, the waters had dried up enough for them to see the tops of high mountains.

Forty days later, Noah opened up a window in the ark. He wanted to know if it were safe for them to leave the boat. He let a raven loose to see if it would land somewhere. It flew around and around and looked for dry land.

Then he let out a dove, but it could not find a place to land and it returned to the boat.

Noah and his family leave the ark

SEVEN days later, Noah let the dove loose once more. This time the dove flew out and did not return until that evening. When it came back, it had a fresh olive leaf in its bill. This was a sign to Noah that the waters were going down on the earth.

After another seven days, he let the dove loose once again. This time the dove flew away and did not return. Noah knew that this meant that the dove had found safe land and had decided to stay there. Noah also knew that the flood was now over.

Noah and his family removed the door to the ark. They had been inside the boat for a little more than a year, but now it was safe for them to leave the ark and go out upon the earth. They also brought all the animals out with them.

God blessed all those living creatures that He had saved, both Noah and his family and the animals that they had brought with them on the ark. He told them to be numerous upon the earth and to multiply.

This was almost the same blessing that He had given when He first created living creatures, for this was almost a second creation, a new beginning.

Noah makes a sacrifice to the Lord

ONE of the first things that Noah did when he left the ark was to build an altar. He wanted to thank God for saving him and his family and all the different types of animals that lived upon the earth.

Noah chose a number of animals that were special to the Lord, and he sacrificed them upon his altar. It was a very special sacrifice in which the entire animal was offered to the Lord.

God was very pleased with what Noah had done. God had flooded the earth to take away sin and selfishness, and this was a sign that the new beginning was starting out right. Noah was not being selfish, but rather he realized that it was right for him to thank and worship God.

God was so pleased with Noah that He made a promise to him. He told Noah that He would never again kill all the living things upon the earth as He had done in the flood. He knew that humans were weak and that they would probably sin again, but He would not allow that to change His mind.

One thing had changed upon the earth. All the sins that men and women had committed had caused fear to grow upon the earth so that animals no longer trusted humans as they had before.

God makes a Covenant with Noah and his family

GOD also kept His promise to make a Covenant with Noah and his family. A Covenant is a very special promise of love and protection, and that is what God wanted to give to Noah.

God told Noah that He would never again send such a terrible flood upon the earth. He would also give Noah a sign of His Covenant. God placed a rainbow in the sky and said that this would be a reminder for all times that He would never again destroy all the earth with a flood.

Every time that we look up into the sky after it has rained and we see the beautiful colors of a rainbow, we can remember how much God loves us. It is a promise that He will protect us and keep us safe in His love. It is also a promise that even if bad things do happen in our lives, all we have to do is call upon Him and He will be there for us.

The most important way that God fulfilled His promise is when He sent His only Son Jesus into the world. Jesus gave us a new sign of God's love, the Cross, so that we could be saved from the flood of sins and evil and selfishness that surrounds us.

Noah plants a vineyard

WHEN Noah and his family had finished their sacrifice, they went out into the land to begin their new lives. They planted gardens and tended sheep and cattle.

God blessed them all, and they had many children and grandchildren. Soon the entire face of the earth was covered with their descendants.

Noah decided that he wanted to be a farmer, and he planted some grape vines for himself. One day he let the grape juice get too old, and it became wine. Noah had never seen wine before, and he drank too much of it and fell asleep in his tent.

The sons of Noah went into their father's tent and saw their father asleep without clothes on. One of the sons laughed at his father and made fun of him, even though what had happened was not really Noah's fault. The other two sons were respectful, and they covered up their father and quietly went out of the tent.

When Noah awoke, he heard of what had happened. He blessed the two sons who had done what is right and who had shown him respect, but he cursed the family of the son who had treated him so poorly.

David is pleased with the Noah story

A ND so the story of Noah ends sadly. Even though God had taken such good care of Noah and his family, one of Noah's sons began to sin almost immediately after the flood. We would have to wait for Jesus to come upon the earth to free us from our sins for all time.

When David and all his court heard this story, they were very pleased. David saw how this story showed God's great love for us. It also showed that sin brings terrible things upon the earth. Once it brought a flood that punished the whole earth, but even now it brought terrible pain and hurt and sadness upon the earth.

Possibly the worst effect of our sins is the knowledge that we have turned our backs upon God and upon those whom we do not know.

David decided that this story should be told to all peoples of every age. He told his court scribes, the people who knew how to write, to copy it down. It would become part of the holy books that David was collecting—the beginning of what we call the Bible.

Thus, the story, like the rainbow, became an eternal sign of God's love for us.

Dear Parents,

The story of Noah and the flood is one of the most familiar of the Bible stories we teach our children. It has a valuable mix of justice and mercy that they need to hear.

Our children need to hear of justice to learn that their sins do have an effect in their lives. Sin brings chaos into our lives (for the flood is a symbol of the return of the chaos and evil upon the earth). One only need think of how sin and selfishness isolate us from those whom we should love. A lie or a betrayal destroys the trust we should have for each other. Violence or using and manipulating people means I treat another as if he/she were an object and thus become like a vicious animal myself. Whatever the sin, the end result is to bring sadness and hurt into the world — a flood of pain.

But God shows mercy to Noah and his family by saving them from the flood. Then He shows mercy to all of creation by offering it His Covenant. What He began then, He fulfilled in Christ, who like the rainbow, is a beacon of God's mercy. His Cross becomes the ark that saves us from the flood of sin that surrounds us.

Shalom
Fr. Jude Winkler, OFM Conv.